MW01535279

kinsey

La collection design&designer est éditée par
PYRAMYD ntcv
15, rue de Turbigo
75002 Paris – France

Tél. : 33 (0) 1 40 26 00 99
Fax : 33 (0) 1 40 26 00 79
www.pyramyd-editions.com

©PYRAMYD ntcv, 2006
All artworks©Kinsey, 2006

Direction éditoriale : Michel Chanaud, Patrick Morin, Céline Remechido
Suivi éditorial : Céline Remechido assistée d'Émilie Lamy
Traduction de la préface : Jean-René Étienne
Correction français : Paula Gouveia-Pinheiro
Correction anglais : Paul Jones
Portrait de la couverture : George Trumbull
Conception graphique de la collection : Super Cinq
Conception graphique du livre : Alex Viougeas
Conception graphique de la couverture : Pyramyd ntcv

Tous droits réservés.
Toute reproduction ou transmission, même partielle, sous quelque forme que ce soit, est interdite sans autorisation écrite du détenteur des droits.

ISBN : 2-35017-020-9
ISSN : 1636-8150
Dépôt légal : 1er trimestre 2006

Imprimé en Italie par Eurografica

kinsey

préfacé par shana nys dambrot

KINSEY & KINSEY

Son enfance dans les années soixante-dix et quatre-vingt, Kinsey l'a passée tout entière dans le nord-est des États-Unis (Pittsburgh, Delaware, Jersey), à l'exception d'une merveilleuse parenthèse de quatre ans en Californie où il a laissé son cœur. La première carrière de ce grand escogriffe à coupe afro mordu de voyages a touché le fond quand il s'est retrouvé à « décaper à la sableuse, en plein soleil, des transformateurs gros comme des éléphants. Ça t'est déjà arrivé de trouver du sable dans ton cul ? Si non, tu sais pas ta chance. » Il n'est donc pas étonnant qu'il ait atterri sur les bancs d'une école d'art (étudiant l'illustration à l'Art Institute of Pittsburgh et le design à celui d'Atlanta) avant de tracer la route, et de s'arrêter finalement à San Diego pour fonder BLK/MRKT en 1996. Kinsey conserve un lien étroit avec la rue et la ville, ses premières sources d'inspiration et d'énergie, et il est incontestable que son travail est marqué par l'immédiateté et l'urgence du vernaculaire brut griffonné sur les murs, mais ses images ne procèdent pas, et n'ont jamais procédé, de cette seule dynamique. Son attachement aux palettes les plus lyriques et aux récits symboliques riches en émotion et en psycho-

Growing up mostly in the Northeastern United States (Pittsburgh, Delaware, Jersey) in the 1970s and '80s – except for four blissful years in California where he left his heart – Kinsey was a tall, lanky kid with a fro and a bit of a traveling Jones, whose previous employment hit a low point while "sandblasting transformers the size of elephants in the hot sun. You ever find sand in your ass? Well, it sucks." So perhaps it's not surprising that he ended up first attending art school (illustration at The Art Institute of Pittsburgh and design at The Art Institute of Atlanta), and then hitting the road, eventually founding BLK/MRKT in San Diego in 1996. Kinsey has a personal affinity for the urban street as the original energetic inspiration of his art, and the immediacy and urgency of the scrawled outsider vernacular is certainly present in his work, but it is not now nor has it ever been the only dynamic operating in his images. His commitment to lyrical palettes, emotionally and psychologically charged symbolic narratives, and the development of a broad lexicon of surface qualities, types of brushwork, styles of representation and art-historical references all contribute to the depth and lasting impact of the paintings – hybrids that are, as with so much in Kinsey's world, more than the sum of their parts.

logie, son développement d'un vaste vocabulaire de textures, de factures, de styles et de références à l'histoire de l'art contribuent à la profondeur, à l'impact et à la longévité de ses tableaux, ces hybrides qui sont, comme c'est souvent le cas dans l'univers de Kinsey, plus que la somme de leurs parties.
Kinsey a le don de garder plusieurs fréquences de communication ouvertes en même temps et toutes ses entreprises en profitent grandement. Sa sensibilité visuelle exacerbée est foncièrement duelle, elle circule librement entre les beaux-arts et le design commercial. Un milieu conceptuel aussi poreux que le sien fonctionne comme sa propre main : en alliant une certaine sophistication classique à une rudesse tout urbaine, postindustrielle. De fait, son style croise l'art de la rue et celui des musées, le public et le privé, la communication à son plus fonctionnel et le design à son plus formel. Ses tableaux sont à la fois précis et ambigus, ils parviennent à porter un message clair tout en continuant à déployer leur sens au fil du temps. Les personnages récurrents qui les peuplent sont devenus reconnaissables au premier coup d'œil. Ils tournent souvent le dos au spectateur, posture dramatique presque littérairement métaphorique, dont le contenu émotionnel nous est immédiatement accessible.

He has a capacity for keeping several channels of communication open at once that serves him well in all of his pursuits. Kinsey's passionate visual sensibility is rooted in duality, freely crisscrossing the border between fine art and commercial design. The way a conceptually porous environment like Kinsey's works is the way his own hand works: with both a rarefied, academic quality and a raw, post-industrial urbanity. In fact his style is itself a kind of hybrid between high and low, public and private, communicative function and pure design. He makes paintings that are both crisp and ambiguous, both communicating clearly and continuing to unfold and deepen over time. His recurring characters have become instantly recognizable. Often their backs are to the viewer, a dramatic gesture with almost literary metaphoric quality instantly accessible to the viewer in terms of emotional meaning. Kinsey describes the inspiration this way: "I like to represent the human condition in both abstract forms inspired by the city environment I currently reside in as well as representational iconography. If I lived in the mountains, I'm sure I'd have trees and elements of nature as abstract background subject matter." Well, in that case, what might we see next? Wine jugs, palm trees, stone bridges, pagodas, banyans?

Kinsey en décrit ainsi l'inspiration : « J'aime représenter la condition humaine en puisant à la fois dans les formes abstraites que me souffle la ville qui m'entoure et dans une iconographie figurative. Si je vivais à la montagne, je parie qu'en guise d'arrière-plan abstrait à mes peintures j'aurais des motifs naturels. » Qui sait ce que nous réserve l'avenir ? Verrons-nous des pichets de vin, des palmiers, des ponts de pierre, des pagodes, des banians ?
Pour l'heure, ce sont ses expositions qui lui dictent son itinéraire ; en 2006 ce sera Londres, la Belgique et la Suisse. Comme je ne vis pas en ermite, cela fait des années que je vois les réalisations publiques et/ou commerciales de Kinsey et BLK/MRKT et depuis l'ouverture, l'an dernier, de sa galerie à Culver City, je connais l'homme personnellement (par exemple, je sais que lui et sa partenaire en affaires et en amour, Jana DesForges, possèdent un cochon domestique dont le nom complet est Marguerite Del Encino). Pourtant, j'ignorais qu'il jouissait d'une telle reconnaissance à l'étranger. Son travail fait l'objet, en plus des expositions, de nombreux articles et publications. Kinsey était déjà connu au moment de son triomphe à la Galerie Magda Danysz à Paris en 2001, sans parler, depuis, de son exposition à l'Urbis Museum de Manchester et sans compter l'engouement des médias de l'art, du design

For now, Kinsey's travel is prescribed by the itinerary of his paintings, with exhibitions of his fine art coming up in London, Belgium and Switzerland in 2006. Although I, like everyone else who leaves their houses, have been aware of Kinsey and BLK/MRKT's public/commercial projects for years and have personally known Kinsey since the gallery opened in Culver City last year (for example, I know that the full name of the pet pig he keeps with life and business partner Jana DesForges is Marguerite Del Encino), I had no idea he had garnered so much attention internationally. Apparently, he gets a lot of coverage in magazines and books in addition to the exhibitions. He was already well known by the time of his wildly popular 2001 exhibition in Paris at Magda Danysz Gallery, not to mention his 2004 show at the Urbis Museum in Manchester, and that's not even counting all the love from the art, design and lifestyle media in Thailand, Singapore, Hong Kong, Japan and even Russia. He's also in demand as a speaker in New York advertising circles, the American Institute of Graphic Arts, Art Center in Pasadena, UCLA and in his own studio.
Sounds like a charmed life, so I couldn't help asking, was he happy most of the time? "I try to be. It's

et du *lifestyle* en Thaïlande, à Singapour, à Hong Kong, au Japon et jusqu'en Russie. Et ses talents de conférencier sont très demandés dans les milieux new-yorkais de la publicité, à l'American Institute of Graphic Arts, à l'Art Center de Pasadena, à UCLA ainsi que dans son propre studio.
Idyllique, non ? Je n'ai pas pu m'empêcher de lui demander s'il était globalement heureux. « J'essaie. Le monde n'est pas facile à vivre. Parfois même, assez douloureux. J'aime vraiment la Californie. On ne peut pas être plus près du paradis sans se retirer du monde. » Et la galerie ? La présence d'une galerie ouverte au public au rez-de-chaussée de ses bureaux et la circulation accrue de visiteurs et d'artistes qu'elle induit influencent-elles sa réflexion sur le design ? « Sans aucun doute. Tous les artistes ont une vision différente de l'art et cette diversité est une grande source d'inspiration. Tenir une galerie permet un rapport très personnel aux artistes et à leurs démarches, parfois trop personnel.»
Le nouveau bâtiment est lui-même lisible comme une métaphore de la sensibilité créative de Kinsey. Jana et lui ont repéré le potentiel d'un lieu urbain en déshérence – une usine d'épices désaffectée où ils ont édifié leur empire de l'image. À l'étage, un labyrinthe de sols moquettés et de parois de verre abrite l'agence de design BLK/MRKT. Au-dessous, une galerie d'art classique, à l'européenne,

hard to live in this world. It can be painful at times. I really do like California. It's the closest place to paradise without being isolated from the outside world." What about the gallery? Has having a public art gallery on the first floor influenced his thinking about design in terms of the heightened flow of people and artists through the space? "Yes indeed. Looking at people's different approaches to art is really inspiring. Having a gallery really gives you a personal experience with the artists and their processes, sometimes too personal."
The new building is itself a kind of metaphor for Kinsey's creative sensibility. He and Jana saw the potential in the once-gutted urban space – a defunct spice factory actually – and built up from that to a self-contained image empire. Upstairs is the soft-carpeted labyrinth of glass-walled rooms that houses the BLK/MRKT design firm. Downstairs is a classic European-style fine art gallery outfitted in sealed concrete, eggshell white latex and track-lighting. This gallery hosts rotating exhibitions of painting, sculpture and installation from a group of artists who, like Kinsey, are loosely bound by various allegiances to the world of graffiti and street-side art. Yet, also like Kinsey, artists as diverse as Tiffany

habillée de béton vernis, de latex coquille d'œuf et de spots sur rail. Là se tiennent les expositions de peinture, sculpture et installation d'un groupe d'artistes qui sont, à l'instar de Kinsey, affiliés à divers titres et degrés au monde du graffiti et du street art. Mais, aussi différents que soient Tiffany Bozic, David Choe ou Jose Parla, tous partagent bien plus que l'esthétique urbaine de leurs débuts : ils prennent très au sérieux l'aspect technique de leur travail de studio, se référant constamment à l'histoire de l'art et construisant un discours sociopolitique tout en développant leur technique avec zèle. Kinsey prévoit d'exposer ses propres productions à la galerie en septembre 2006 et il s'intégrera parfaitement à leur programme esthétique. Supportant les éléments figuratifs expressifs, les somptueuses surfaces picturales de Kinsey animent l'arrière-fond de ses figures monolithiques, tout en textures fondues et rubans de couleur filant à hauteur d'yeux, motifs faits d'air et de mouvement. Ces morceaux de peinture affichent une assurance, une maturité et une détermination qui engage à la fois l'espace de la toile et les concepts de la peinture d'avant-garde. Ils font montre d'une application, d'une gravité, rare parmi les jeunes artistes d'aujourd'hui et d'autant plus inattendue qu'elle se trouve au croisement physique et stylistique de l'art et du commerce.

Bozic, David Choe and Jose Parla share more than a formative urban aesthetic. They all take the craftsmanship of their studio work very seriously, looking at art history and articulating sociopolitical narrative while diligently developing atelier technique. Kinsey plans to show his own work at the gallery in September of 2006, and it fits right in with their aesthetic program. Anchoring the expressive figurative elements are Kinsey's luxurious painterly surfaces that enliven the space behind his monolithic figures; their blurred textures and swaths of color sweeping past at eye level, make patterns out of air and motion. These painterly passages have a mature confidence and resolve to them that engage both pictorial space and concepts of avant-garde painting. It's a studiousness, a gravitas, that has not been common among artists of the younger generations, and which is all the more unexpected for being stylistically and physically located at a nexus of art and commerce.
Advertising itself is a hybrid social science, part mechanistic formula, part cultural anthropology, and commissions at BLK/MRKT are about problem-solving, not compromise. The domain of the graphic designer straddles the border between form (pure, private, innovative creativity) and function (efficient,

La publicité elle-même est une science sociale hybride, participant à la fois d'un savoir-faire tout mécanique et d'une forme d'anthropologie culturelle, et dans son travail de commande, BLK/MRKT ne recherche que les solutions graphiques, pas le compromis. Le graphisme est à cheval sur la frontière qui sépare la forme (la créativité pure, personnelle, novatrice) de la fonction (la communication dans son effort d'efficace, de persuasion et de précision). S'il est donc logique que les meilleurs designers soient ceux qui manient aussi bien les deux idiomes, Kinsey prouve de manière éclatante que ce bilinguisme sert également la cause de l'art avec un grand A. « Commercialement, mon objectif me vient de l'extérieur : satisfaire les besoins du client et de la marque ou du message qu'il souhaite diffuser. Mon travail personnel me permet de m'accomplir, en ayant satisfait un objectif 100 % personnel. Le dénominateur commun aux deux démarches c'est l'intégrité. J'aime travailler ces deux aspects. J'en tire une grande latitude d'expérimentation et d'exploration. »

BLK/MRKT refuse régulièrement de se mettre au service de sociétés ou de produits qui, pour des raisons diverses, morales ou esthétiques, ne leur inspirent pas confiance. Le client digne de l'agence ne cherche pas à s'attacher des publicitaires standards, mais un studio capable d'un véritable travail

persuasive, specific communication). It stands to reason that the best designers would be those with a facility for both, but as Kinsey amply demonstrates, ambidexterity with these idioms serves the cause of serious fine art just as well. "Commercially, I have an outside objective; that being the facilitation of our client's needs and the needs of the brand or message they wish to convey. Personally, I create work that enables me to walk away happy, the objective being 100% personal. In both there is a commonality in integrity. I like working both sides. It gives me a lot of room for experimentation and exploration."

BLK/MRKT regularly turns down jobs for companies or products they don't feel good about for reasons that vary from moral to aesthetic suspicions. A true BLK/MRKT client is not looking for the usual advertising suspects, but rather for a firm that can deliver genuine artistry. Even, or especially, high-profile accounts and commissions for Absolut, Adidas, DC Shoes, Timex, Hotel des Arts and Apple pursue a sensibility of bohemian creative expression that can charm even the most sophisticated, urbane consumer. These firms want the real avant-garde, the kind that can't be faked. But they also need to

d'artiste. Même, ou surtout, leurs comptes et contrats les plus prestigieux, tels Absolut, Adidas, DC Shoes, Timex, Hotel des Arts ou Apple, visent une sensibilité « arty » et créative apte à séduire le client le plus sophistiqué et raffiné. Ce que veulent ces firmes, c'est l'avant-garde, le vrai, celui qu'on ne peut pas imiter. Mais elles doivent aussi pouvoir compter sur des professionnels responsables, sur le talent desquels elles misent des millions de dollars de profit potentiel. C'est là un ensemble hybride et peu d'entreprises correspondent au créneau mais l'excellence de BLK/MRKT est reconnue par tous. Depuis la première agence fondée à San Diego, et plus encore aujourd'hui, après le déménagement à Los Angeles et la création de la galerie, Kinsey a toujours travaillé à jeter des ponts entre le monde de l'entreprise et celui de la contre-culture, son ennemi juré. Ainsi, il offre aux artistes une tribune et même un revenu qui leur permettent de travailler sans sacrifier leur point de vue.

Shana Nys Dambrot
Los Angeles

be able to rely on their designers as mature professionals on whose work millions of sales dollars are potentially staked. It's a hybrid gestalt, and there are very few of these companies that fit the bill, but BLK/MRKT is universally acknowledged to be one of the very best in the game. From the original company based in San Diego and now even more with the move to LA and the founding of the gallery, Kinsey's work has always been about bridging the gap between corporate culture and its entrenched adversary, counter-culture; and, in the process, providing a forum and even an income for artists to work without compromising their visions.

Shana Nys Dambrot
Los Angeles

BLK/MRKT
CREATIVE VISUAL COMMUNICATION
BLK/MRKT
CREATIVE VISUAL COMMUNICATION
BLK/MRKT
CREATIVE VISUAL COMMUNICATION
BLK/MRKT

SNIPER BLK/MRKT
PHOTOGRAPHIE : MONICA HOOVER
ÉTATS-UNIS, 1999

BLK/MRKT SNIPER
PHOTOGRAPH: MONICA HOOVER
USA, 1999

LOGO BLK/MRKT
IDENTITÉ VISUELLE
ÉTATS-UNIS, 2003

BLK/MRKT LOGO
CORPORATE IDENTITY
USA, 2003

TRUTH CAMPAIGN
CAMPAGNE DE PRÉVENTION
CONTRE LE TABAC
CLIENT : CRISPIN PORTER + BOGUSKY
PHOTOGRAPHIE : ANGELA BOATWRIGHT
4 x 8 M PAPIER, LATEX ACRYLIQUE ET
BOMBE DE PEINTURE, ÉTATS-UNIS, 2001

TRUTH CAMPAIGN
SMOKING AWARENESS CAMPAIGN
CLIENT: CRISPIN PORTER + BOGUSKY
PHOTOGRAPH: ANGELA BOATWRIGHT
15' x 25'
PAPER, ACRYLIC LATEX AND SPRAY PAINT
USA, 2001

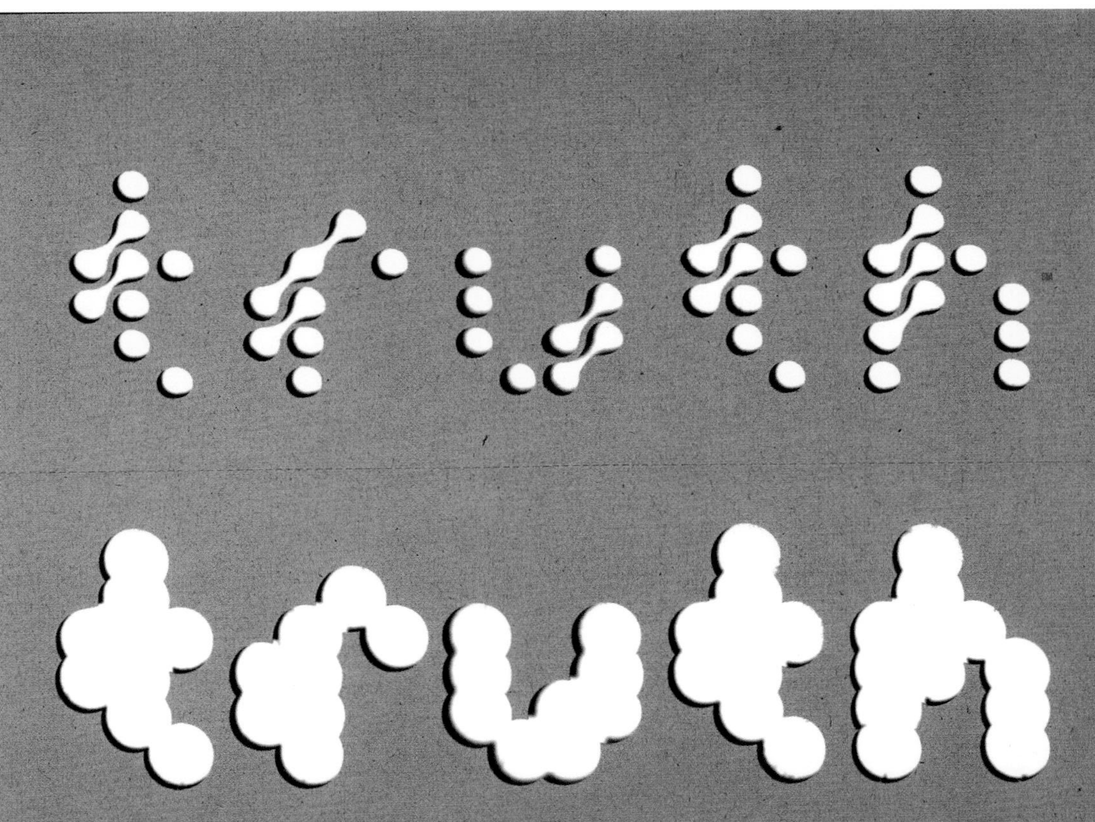
truth
truth
Punch out letters. Separate at perfs. Use big stencil for background. Use another color for small stencil. Repeat until Big Tobacco starts telling the truth.

PAPIER ET COLLE
LOS ANGELES, 2000

PAPER AND WHEAT PASTE
LOS ANGELES, 2000

PAPIER ET COLLE
PARIS, 2001

PAPER AND WHEAT PASTE
PARIS, 2001

PAPIER ET COLLE
LOS ANGELES, 2003

PAPER AND WHEAT PASTE
LOS ANGELES, 2003

PHOTOGRAPHIE : MICHAEL BALLARD
LOS ANGELES, 2003

PHOTOGRAPH: MICHAEL BALLARD
LOS ANGELES, 2003

CAMPAGNE D'AFFICHAGE POUR HEINEKEN
CLIENT : PUBLICIS USA
ILLUSTRATION
ÉTATS-UNIS, 2004

OUTDOOR CAMPAIGN FOR HEINEKEN
CLIENT: PUBLICIS USA
ILLUSTRATION
USA, 2004

RESPECT.
CLEARCHANNEL
AVAILABLE
DORIN
627-0007

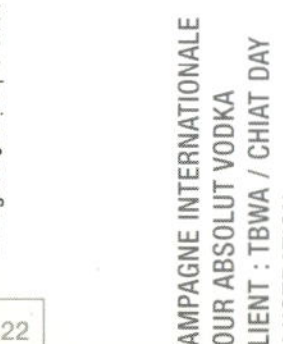

WORLDWIDE CAMPAIGN
FOR ABSOLUT VODKA
CLIENT: TBWA / CHIAT DAY
ILLUSTRATION
2004

CAMPAGNE INTERNATIONALE
POUR ABSOLUT VODKA
CLIENT : TBWA / CHIAT DAY
ILLUSTRATION
2004

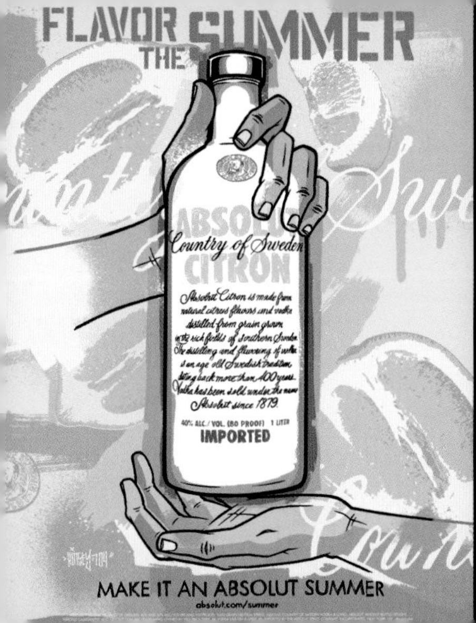

FLAVOR THE SUMMER

ABSOLUT
Country of Sweden
CITRON

Absolut Citron is made from
natural citrus flavors and vodka
distilled from grain grown
in the rich fields of southern Sweden.
The distilling and flavoring of vodka
is an age old Swedish tradition
dating back more than 400 years.
Vodka has been sold under the name
Absolut since 1879.

40% ALC./VOL. (80 PROOF) 1 LITER
IMPORTED

MAKE IT AN ABSOLUT SUMMER
absolut.com/summer

FLAVOR THE SUMMER

COUNTRY OF SWEDEN
ABSOLUT

ABSOLUT
Country of Sweden
VANILIA

IMPORTED

MAKE IT AN ABSOLUT SUMMER
absolut.com/summer

K
RE INK
PONDER - REASON Z FORMU ATE - ELEVATE

RETHINK FATHER
90 x 60 CM
IMPRESSION OFFSET
ÉTATS-UNIS, 1999

RETHINK FATHER
36" x 24"
OFFSET PRINT
USA, 1999

UNLEARN
36" x 24"
OFFSET PRINT
USA, 1999

UNLEARN
90 x 60 CM
IMPRESSION OFFSET
ÉTATS-UNIS, 1999

ONTAGIOUS
28
COUNT

POST CONSUMED
FILL IN THE BLANK.

PAGES 28-29 :
CONTAGIOUS
228 x 122 CM
ACRYLIQUE, PAPIER, HUILE ET BOMBE DE PEINTURE SUR DES OBJETS TROUVÉS
ÉTATS-UNIS, 2003

PAGES 28-29:
CONTAGIOUS
90" x 48"
ACRYLIC, PAPER, OIL AND SPRAY PAINT ON FOUND OBJECTS
USA, 2003

BLANK X, POST CONSUMED & UNRESTED
(DE GAUCHE À DROITE)
122 x 60 CM
ACRYLIQUE, PAPIER, HUILE ET BOMBE DE PEINTURE SUR DES OBJETS TROUVÉS
ÉTATS-UNIS, 2003

BLANK X, POST CONSUME & UNRESTED
(FROM LEFT TO RIGHT)
48" x 24"
ACRYLIC, PAPER, OIL AND SPRAY PAINT ON FOUND OBJECTS
USA, 2003

FORGET RELEASE
228 x 60 CM
ACRYLIQUE, HUILE ET BOMBE DE PEINTURE
SUR UNE PORTE EN BOIS
ÉTATS-UNIS, 2000

FORGET RELEASE
90" x 24"
ACRYLIC, OIL AND SPRAY PAINT
ON WOOD DOOR
USA, 2000

RITUAL LA EVENT PIECE
228 x 122 CM
ACRYLIQUE, HUILE ET BOMBE DE PEINTURE
SUR UN PANNEAU DE BOIS
ETATS-UNIS, 2000

RITUAL LA EVENT PIECE
90" x 48"
ACRYLIC, OIL AND SPRAY PAINT
ON WOOD PANELS
USA, 2000

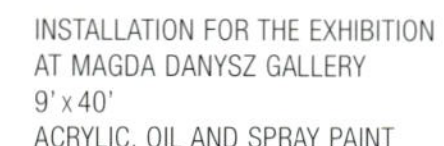

INSTALLATION POUR L'EXPOSITION
À LA GALERIE MAGDA DANYSZ
3 x 12 M
ACRYLIQUE, HUILE ET BOMBE DE PEINTURE
FRANCE, 2000

INSTALLATION FOR THE EXHIBITION
AT MAGDA DANYSZ GALLERY
9' x 40'
ACRYLIC, OIL AND SPRAY PAINT
FRANCE, 2000

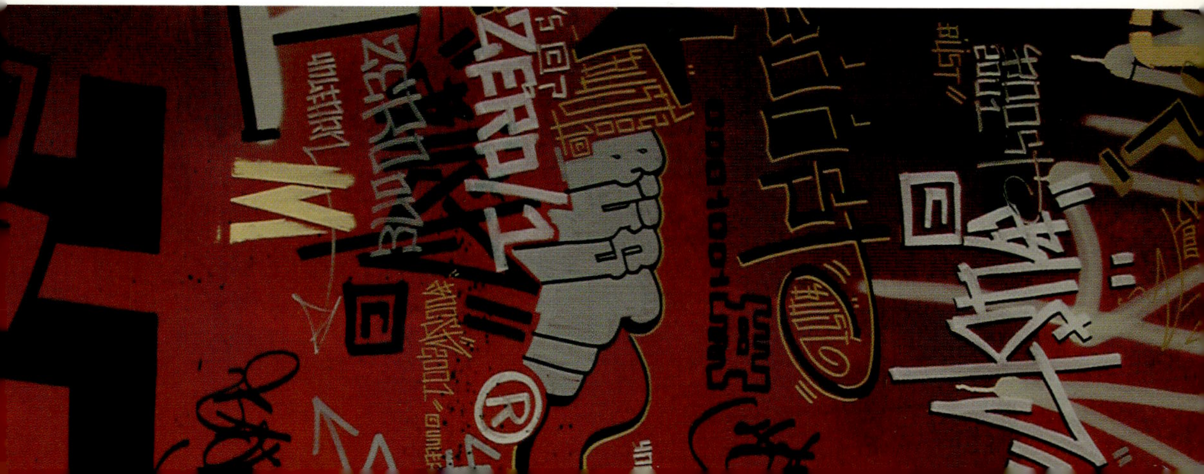

ROGRAM
OUGHT"
ABIT!?
UNLEARN
1992
"BUST"

SIR SPLENDID
POCHETTE DE CD POUR MARCUS B
ILLUSTRATION
USA, 2004

SIR SPLENDID
CD COVER FOR MARCUS B
ILLUSTRATION
USA, 2004

BLACK EYED PEAS, ELEPHUNK LOGO
CLIENT : INTERSCOPE, A&M
ÉTATS-UNIS, 2003

BLACK EYED PEAS, ELEPHUNK LOGO
CLIENT: INTERSCOPE, A&M
USA, 2003

GAGLE « BIG BANG THEORY »
CLIENT : JAZZY SPORT PRODUCTIONS
LOGO, POCHETTE DE CD ET PACKAGING
JAPON, 2005

GAGLE "BIG BANG THEORY"
CLIENT: JAZZY SPORT PRODUCTIONS
LOGO, CD COVER AND PACKAGING
JAPAN, 2005

DUB
PISTOLS

DUB PISTOLS « OFFICIAL CHEMICAL »
CLIENT : GEFFEN RECORDS
LOGO, POCHETTE DE CD ET PACKAGING
ÉTATS-UNIS, 2001

DUB PISTOLS "OFFICIAL CHEMICAL"
CLIENT: GEFFEN RECORDS
LOGO, CD COVER AND PACKAGING
USA, 2001

WICKED ROOTS
IDENTITÉ VISUELLE
ILLUSTRATION
ÉTATS-UNIS, 2004

WICKED ROOTS
CORPORATE IDENTITY
ILLUSTRATION
USA, 2004

HESSEN MOB BOARD
SÉRIGRAPHIE SUR SKATEBOARD
ILLUSTRATION
ALLEMAGNE, 2002

HESSEN MOB BOARD
SCREEN PRINTED SKATEBOARD
ILLUSTRATION
GERMANY, 2002

STRENGTH BOARD
SÉRIGRAPHIE SUR SKATEBOARD
(LES DEUX CÔTÉS)
ÉTATS-UNIS, 2002

STRENGTH BOARD
SCREEN PRINTED SKATEBOARD
(TOP AND BOTTOM)
USA, 2002

UNLEARN
KINSEY © 2002

SCULPTURE
MOULAGE EN POLYRÉSINE ET MÉTAL

SCULPTURE
POLY-RESIN LIQUID METAL COATED CAST

PARIS FREESTYLES
20 x 25 CM
ACRYLIQUE AVEC STYLO ET ENCRE
SUR CARTON
ÉTATS-UNIS, 2001

PARIS FREESTYLES
8" x 10"
ACRYLIC WITH PEN AND INK ON CHIPBOARD
USA, 2001

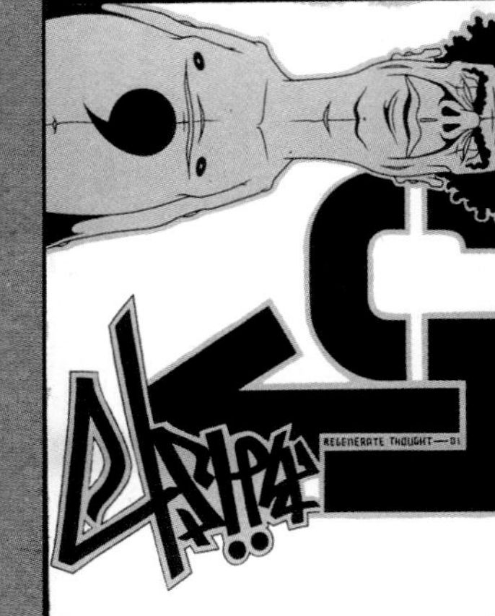

THE GASNER SYNDROME (N° 2 SUR 3)
25 x 20 CM
ACRYLIQUE, PAPIER, STYLO ET ENCRE
SUR CARTON
ÉTATS-UNIS, 2005

THE GASNER SYNDROME (PIECE 2 OF 3)
10" x 8"
ACRYLIC, PAPER WITH PEN AND INK
ON CHIPBOARD
USA, 2005

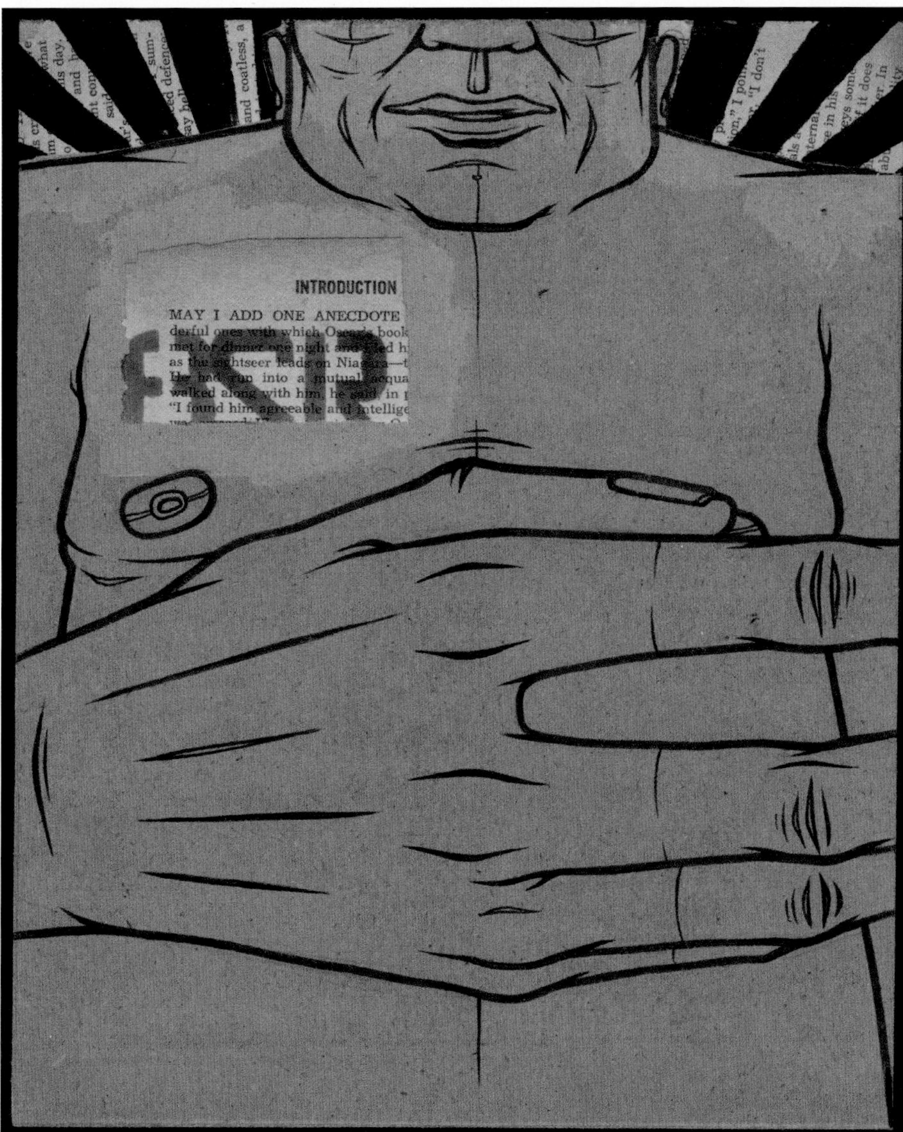
INTRODUCTION
MAY I ADD ONE ANECDOTE
"I found him agreeable and intellige

SEXPOSED, FEAR, SOCIALLY ENGINEERED
(DE GAUCHE À DROITE)
60 x 50 CM
SÉRIGRAPHIE SUR PAPIER
ÉTATS-UNIS, 2004

SEXPOSED, FEAR, SOCIALLY ENGINEERED
(LEFT TO RIGHT)
24" x 20"
SCREEN PRINT ON PAPER
USA, 2004

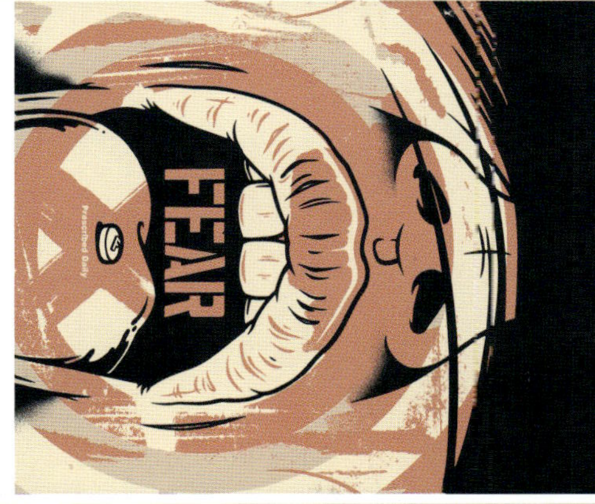

KINSEY
GIANT
2003
5

COLLABORATION KINSEY / GIANT
43 x 28 CM
SÉRIGRAPHIE ET MARQUEUR SUR CARTON
ÉTATS-UNIS, 2003

KINSEY / GIANT COLLABORATION
17" x 11"
SCREEN PRINTING AND MARKER
ON CHIPBOARD
USA, 2003

IN HONOR
20 x 25 CM
ACRYLIQUE, STYLO ET ENCRE SUR CARTON
ÉTATS-UNIS, 2005

IN HONOR
8" x 10"
ACRYLIC WITH PEN AND INK ON CHIPBOARD
USA, 2005

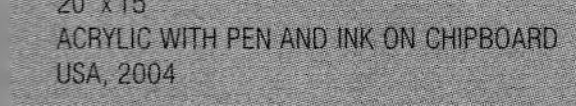

CASH TRIBUTE
50 x 38 CM
ACRYLIQUE, STYLO ET ENCRE SUR CARTON
ÉTATS-UNIS, 2004

CASH TRIBUTE
20" x 15"
ACRYLIC WITH PEN AND INK ON CHIPBOARD
USA, 2004

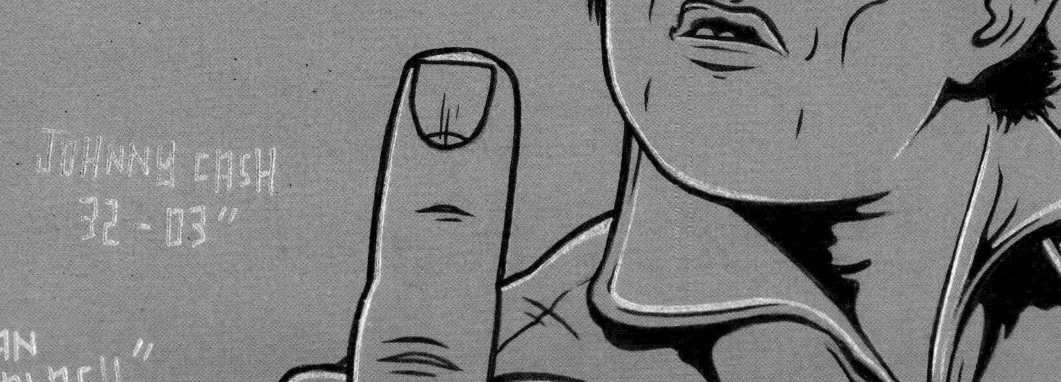

THE THINGS
I HAVE ON
THE BLACK FOR
POOR AND BEATEN
LIVIN' IN THE HOPE
HUNGRY SIDE OF TOWN
WEAR BLACK FOR
WHO NEVER READ
YOU'LL NEVER SEE ME
WEAR A SUIT OF

BASIL HAYWARD GALLERY, PORTLAND OR.
SÉRIGRAPHIE, ACRYLIQUE ET BOMBE
DE PEINTURE SUR DES COUVERTURES
DE LIVRES ET DES POCHETTES
DE DISQUES RÉCUPÉRÉES
ÉTATS-UNIS, 2003

BASIL HAYWARD GALLERY, PORTLAND OR.
SCREEN PRINTING, ACRYLIC AND SPRAY
PAINT ON FOUND BOOK COVERS AND
RECORD SLEEVES
USA, 2003

ALGORITHMS
25 x 30 CM
SÉRIGRAPHIE, SCOTCH, ACRYLIQUE ET BOMBE DE PEINTURE SUR UNE COUVERTURE DE LIVRE RÉCUPÉRÉE
ÉTATS-UNIS, 2003

ALGORITHMS
10" x 12"
SCREEN PRINTING, TAPE, ACRYLIC AND SPRAY PAINT ON FOUND BOOK COVER
USA, 2003

BRASS
30 x 30 CM
SÉRIGRAPHIE SUR UNE POCHETTE DE DISQUE RÉCUPÉRÉE
ÉTATS-UNIS, 2003

BRASS
12" x 12"
SCREEN PRINTING ON FOUND RECORD SLEEVE
USA, 2003

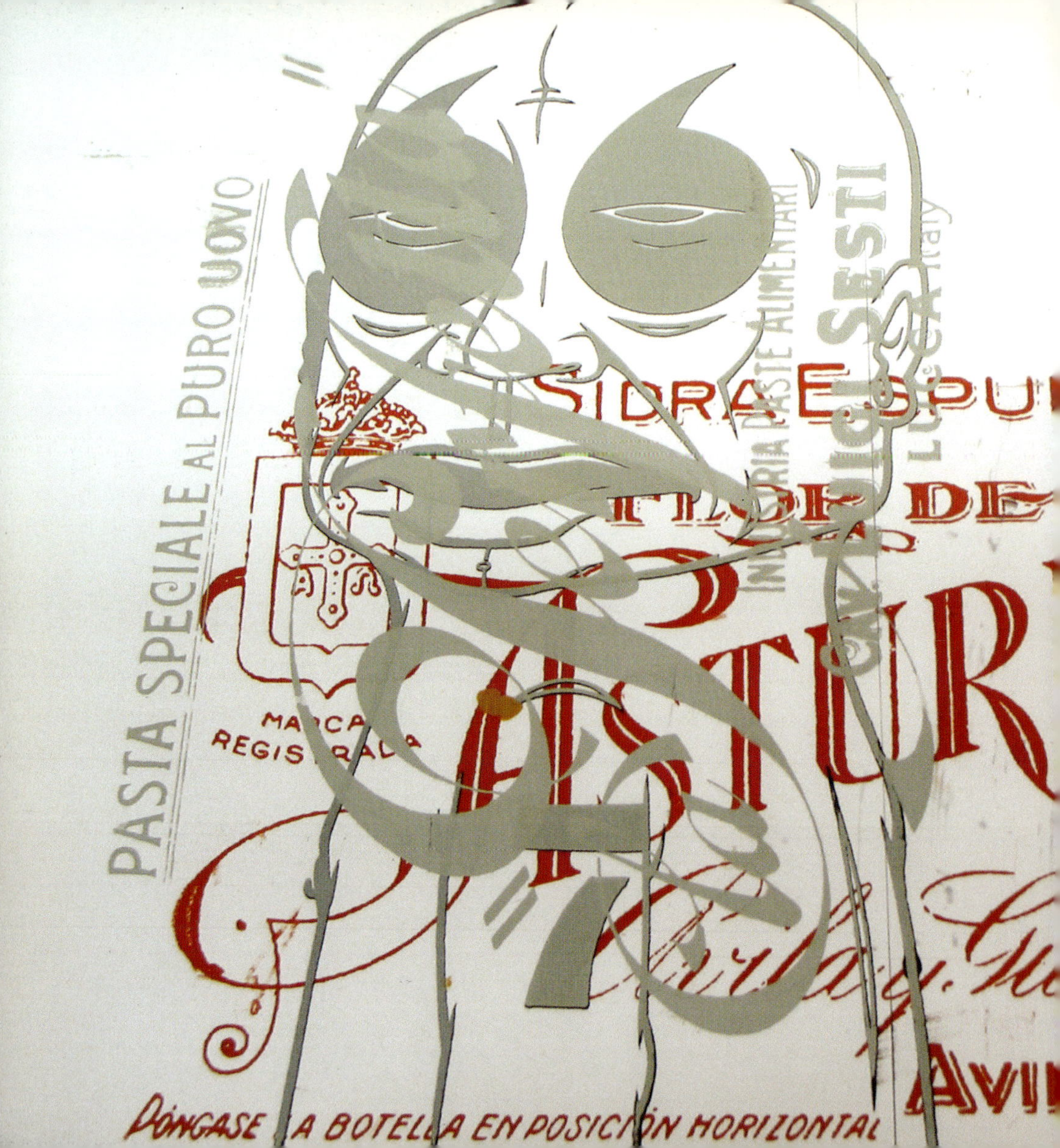

PASTA SPECIALE AL PURO UOVO
MARCA
REGISTRADA
INDUSTRIA PASTE ALIMENTARI
SESTI
PÓNGASE
BOTELLA EN POSICIÓN HORIZONTAL

ESSAI D'IMPRESSION SUR PAPIER
SÉRIGRAPHIE
ÉTATS-UNIS, 2004

TEST PRINT ON PAPER
SCREEN PRINTING
USA, 2004

THIRTY-EIGHT

MAR VISTA BRANCH LIBRARY
WITHDRAWN

COPY 1

309 S342-1

DO NOT REMOVE CARDS FROM POCKET

CARD OWNER IS RESPONSIBLE FOR ALL LIBRARY MATERIAL ISSUED ON HIS CARD

PREVENT DAMAGE – A charge is made for damage to this book or the cards in the pocket.

RETURN BOOKS PROMPTLY – A fine is charged for each day a book is overdue, including Sundays and holidays.

REPORT A LOST BOOK AT ONCE – The charge for a lost book includes the cost of the book plus fines.

LOS ANGELES PUBLIC LIBRARY

Form 36 7-64

JUN 19 1969

WITHDRAWN
18 x 25 CM
SÉRIGRAPHIE, SCOTCH, ACRYLIQUE ET BOMBE DE PEINTURE À L'INTÉRIEUR D'UNE COUVERTURE DE LIVRE RÉCUPÉRÉE
ÉTATS-UNIS, 2003

WITHDRAWN
7" x 10"
SCREEN PRINTING, TAPE, ACRYLIC AND SPRAY PAINT ON FOUND BOOK COVER INSIDE
USA, 2003

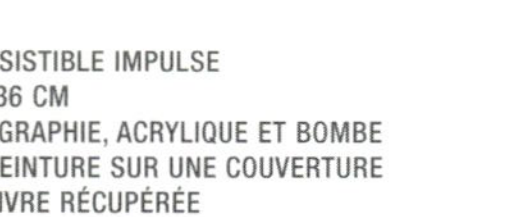

IRRESISTIBLE IMPULSE
22 x 36 CM
SÉRIGRAPHIE, ACRYLIQUE ET BOMBE DE PEINTURE SUR UNE COUVERTURE DE LIVRE RÉCUPÉRÉE
ÉTATS-UNIS, 2003

IRRESISTIBLE IMPULSE
9" x 14"
SCREEN PRINTING, ACRYLIC AND SPRAY PAINT ON FOUND BOOK COVER
USA, 2003

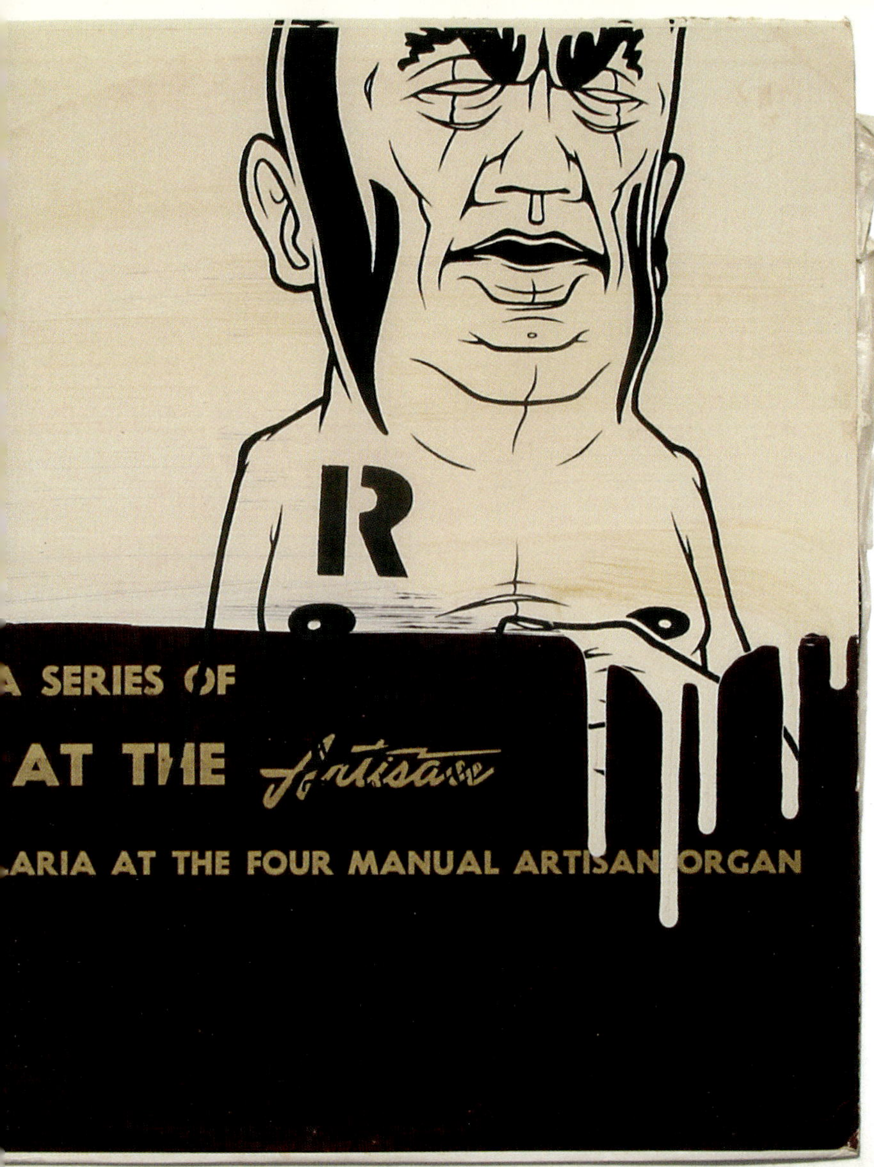

ARTISAN
30 x 30 CM
SÉRIGRAPHIE ET ACRYLIQUE SUR
UNE POCHETTE DE DISQUE RÉCUPÉRÉE
ÉTATS-UNIS, 2003

ARTISAN
12" x 12"
SCREEN PRINTING AND ACRYLIC
ON FOUND RECORD SLEEVE
USA, 2003

IN THE FLESH
18 x 10 CM
STYLO ET ENCRE AVEC PAPIER À
L'INTÉRIEUR D'UNE COUVERTURE DE LIVRE
ÉTATS-UNIS, 2005

IN THE FLESH
7" x 4"
PEN AND INK WITH PAPER ON FOUND BOOK
COVER INSIDE
USA, 2005

REJOICE
30 x 30 CM
SÉRIGRAPHIE, SCOTCH, ACRYLIQUE, STYLO
ET BOMBE DE PEINTURE SUR UNE
POCHETTE DE DISQUE RÉCUPÉRÉE
ÉTATS-UNIS, 2004

REJOICE
12" x 12"
SCREEN PRINTING, TAPE, ACRYLIC, PENCIL
AND SPRAY PAINT ON FOUND RECORD
SLEEVE
USA, 2004

SUPERVISION
22 x 36 CM
SÉRIGRAPHIE ET BOMBE DE PEINTURE SUR
UNE COUVERTURE DE LIVRE RÉCUPÉRÉE
ÉTATS-UNIS, 2004

SUPERVISION
9" x 14"
SCREEN PRINTING AND SPRAY PAINT
ON FOUND BOOK COVER
USA, 2004

HANDBOOK
for Effective Supervision
of Instruction

second
edition

NEAGLEY
and
EVANS

PRENTICE-HA

second editi

HANDBOOK

for
Effective Supervision
of Instruction

7

NEAGLEY and EVANS

PAPIER ET COLLE
PARIS, 1999

PAPER AND WHEAT PASTE
PARIS, 1999

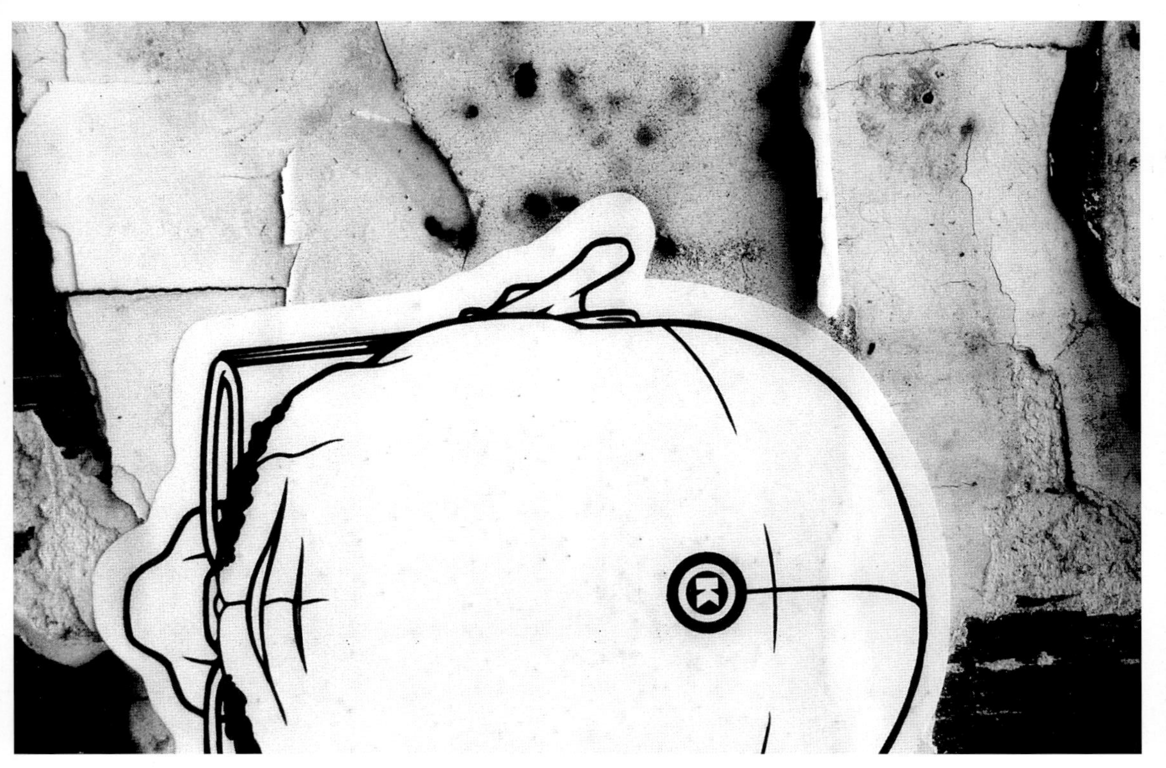

STICKER
FRANCE, 1999

PAPIER ET COLLE
LOS ANGELES, 2004

PAPER AND WHEAT PASTE
LOS ANGELES, 2004

PAPIER ET COLLE
SAN FRANCISCO, 2002

PAPER AND WHEAT PASTE
SAN FRANCISCO, 2002

•MARKET STRE
•YERBA BUENA
PHONE
ABC
FENCES BY
ABC
FENCE CO.
P
PUBLIC
PARKING
$6.00
Evening Special
In after 4PM

EXPOSITION ET INSTALLATION
À LA GALERIE ONE TIME
PHOTOGRAPHIE : DUSTIN BEATTY
ACRYLIQUE ET HUILE
ÉTATS-UNIS, 2002

EXHIBITION AND INSTALLATION
AT THE ONE TIME GALLERY
PHOTOGRAPH: DUSTIN BEATTY
ACRYLIC AND OIL
USA, 2002

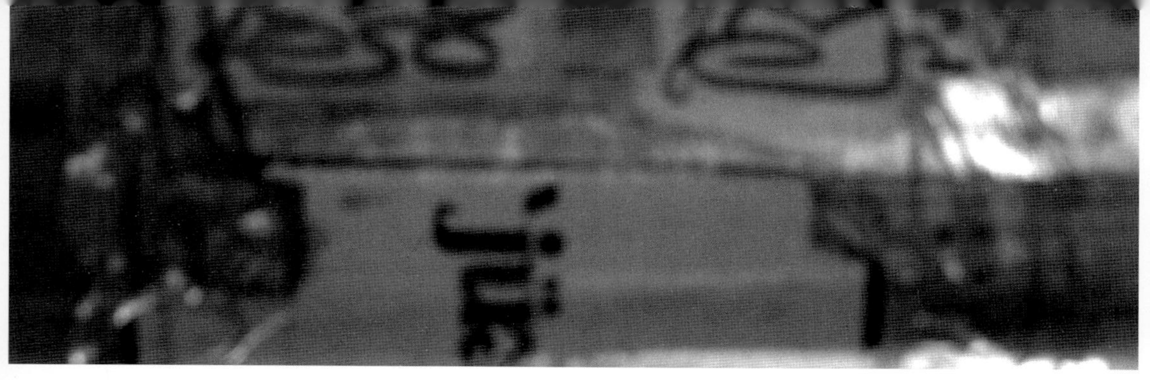

PAPIER ET COLLE
SAN FRANCISCO, 1999

PAPER AND WHEAT PASTE
SAN FRANCISCO, 1999

PAPIER ET COLLE
LOS ANGELES, 2002

PAPER AND WHEAT PASTE
LOS ANGELES, 2002

PAPIER ET COLLE
LOS ANGELES, 2001

PAPER AND WHEAT PASTE
LOS ANGELES, 2001

LASTCALL
The Final Chapter of F. Scott Fitzgerald
MAY 25 SHOWTIME
NO LIMITS
VIACOM

e

PAPIER ET COLLE
LOS ANGELES, 1999

PAPER AND WHEAT PASTE
LOS ANGELES, 1999

152 x 90 CM
PHOTOGRAPHIE : MAVIS
ACRYLIQUE, HUILE ET BOMBE DE PEINTURE
SUR BOIS
ÉTATS-UNIS, 2004

60" x 36"
PHOTOGRAPH: MAVIS
ACRYLIC, OIL AND SPRAY PAINT
ON WOOD
USA, 2004

KISS
DESTINY

HARMONY, RETHINK FATHER, SUFFER
(DE GAUCHE À DROITE)
100 x 76 CM
ACRYLIQUE ET HUILE SUR TOILE
ÉTATS-UNIS, 1999

HARMONY, RETHINK FATHER, SUFFER
(LEFT TO RIGHT)
40" x 30"
ACRYLIC AND OIL ON CANVAS
USA, 1999

PAIN RELIEF
152 x 122 CM
ACRYLIQUE ET HUILE SUR BOIS
ÉTATS-UNIS, 2003

PAIN RELIEF
60" x 48"
ACRYLIC AND OIL ON WOOD
USA, 2003

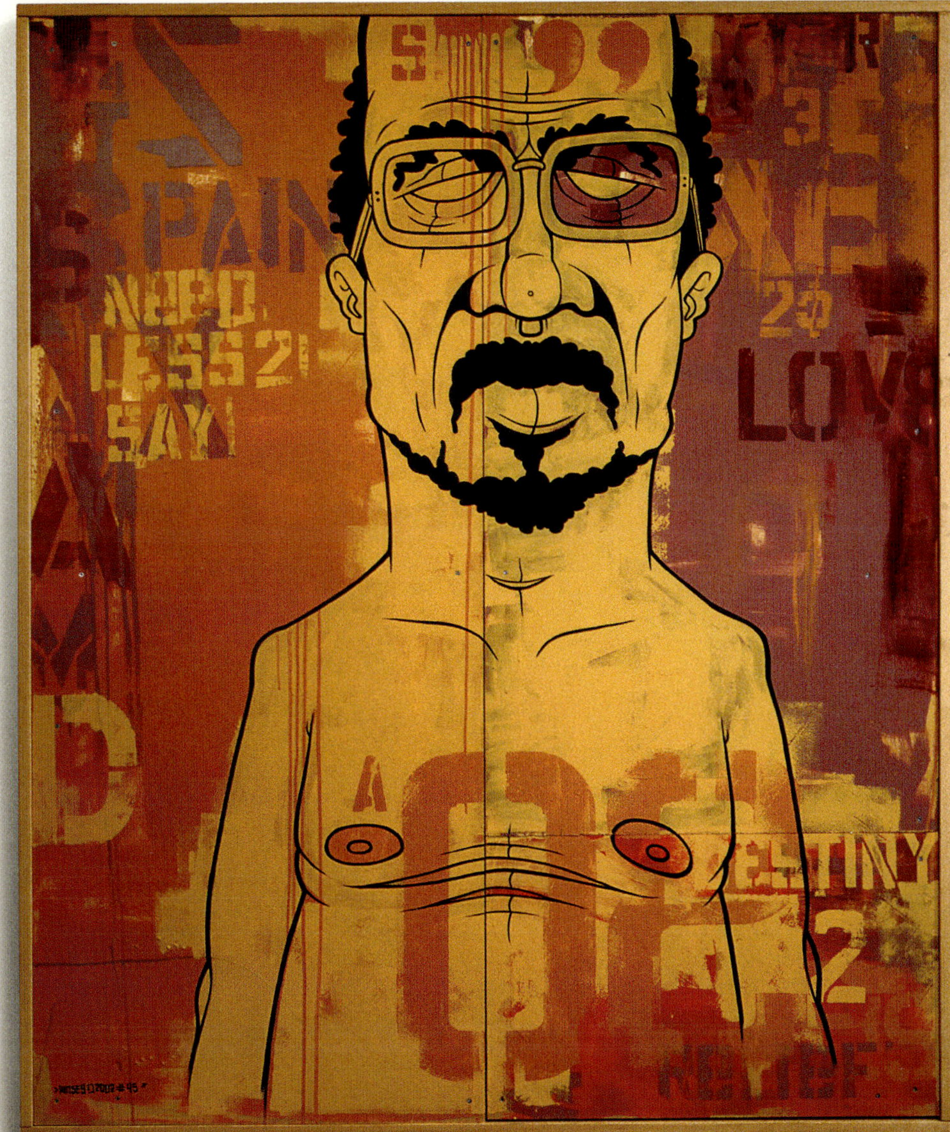
PAIN
NOBO
LESS 2
SAY
LOV
25
DESTINY
2

JEAN JACQUE
60 x 45 CM
SÉRIGRAPHIE
ÉTATS-UNIS, CRÉÉ EN 1999,
IMPRIMÉ EN 2004

JEAN JACQUE
24" x 18"
SCREEN PRINT
USA, CREATED IN 1999,
PRINTED IN 2004

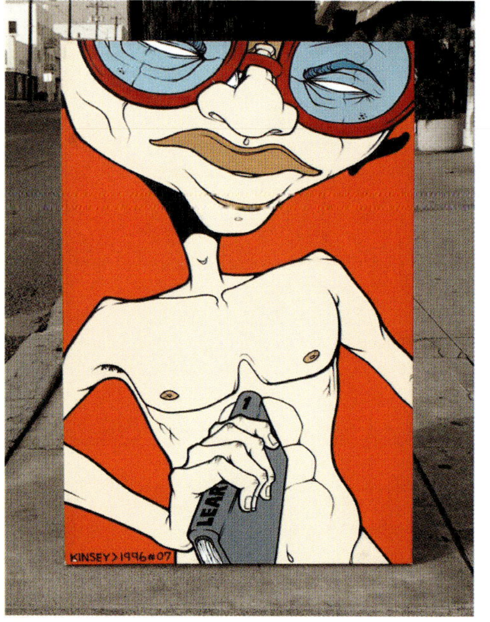

LEARN
90 x 60 CM
ACRYLIQUE ET HUILE SUR TOILE
ÉTATS-UNIS, 1996

LEARN
36" x 24"
ACRYLIC AND OIL ON CANVAS
USA, 1996

NEW ERA
100 x 76 CM
ACRYLIQUE, HUILE SUR TOILE
ÉTATS-UNIS, 1998

NEW ERA
40" x 30"
ACRYLIC, OIL ON CANVAS
USA, 1998

FORM
152 x 76 CM
ACRYLIQUE ET HUILE SUR TOILE
ÉTATS-UNIS, 1997

FORM
60" x 30"
ACRYLIC AND OIL ON CANVAS
USA, 1997

LOGO DC SHOES
IDENTITÉ VISUELLE
ÉTATS-UNIS, 1994

DC SHOES LOGO
CORPORATE IDENTITY
USA, 1994

CAMPAGNE PRESSE DC SHOES
ÉTATS-UNIS, 2001

DC SHOES PRINT CAMPAIGN
USA, 2001

DCSHOECOUSA

DEALER INFO 800-886-8225

WWW.DCSHOECOUSA.COM

METROPOLITAN TERRAIN FOOTWEAR

10 JUIN 2000

BF PT01AD 1502

GOLDIE METALHEADZ LONDON U.K.

MUSIC: DRUM & BASS
PROFESSION: DJ/PRODUCER
CREW: METALHEADZ
AREA: LONDON
SHOES: ASCENT
APPAREL: DC ACTIVE TERRAIN

DCSHOECOUSA

CAMPAGNE DC SHOES
PUBLICITÉ POUR GOLDIE
ÉTATS-UNIS, 2001

DC SHOES CAMPAIGN
GOLDIE PRINT AD
USA, 2001

CAMPAGNE DC SHOES
PUBLICITÉ POUR X-ECUTIONERS
ILLUSTRATION ET DESIGN GRAPHIQUE
ÉTATS-UNIS, 2002

CAMPAGNE DC SHOES
X-ECUTIONERS PRINT AD
ILLUSTRATION AND DESIGN
USA, 2002

KINSEY 2002

FEATURED MODEL: THE BLAZO

EXECUTE INSPIRE

X-ECUTIONERS
DCSHOES

LOUD

SRC

DCSHOECOUSA

TO SEE THE LATEST NEWS, TEAM INFORMATION AND SHOES, VISIT OUR WEB SITE AT WWW.DCSHOECOUSA.COM

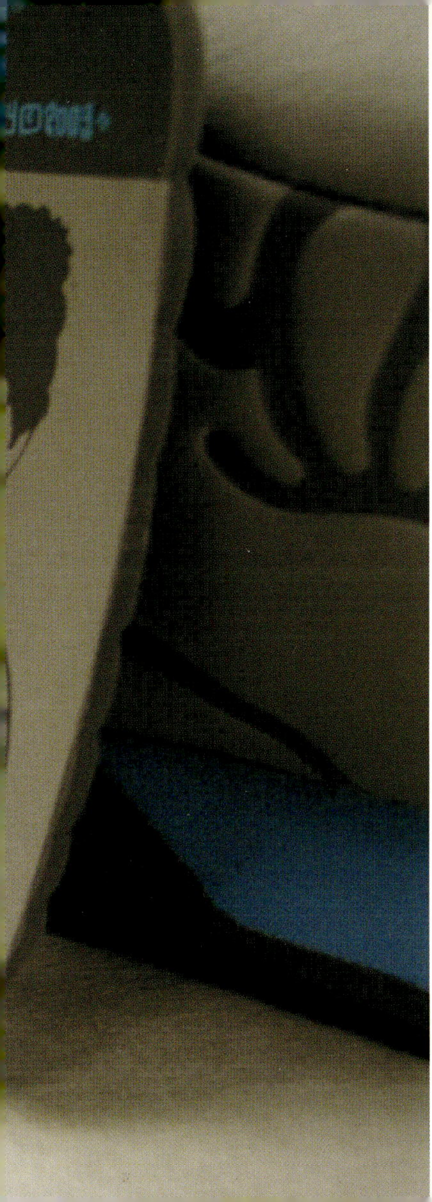

BASKETS CONÇUE PAR KINSEY
POUR DC SHOES ARTIST PROJECTS
BASKETS, PACKAGING ET ÉTIQUETTE
ILLUSTRATION ET DESIGN
ÉTATS-UNIS, 2002

KINSEY SIGNATURE SHOE FOR DC SHOES
ARTIST PROJECTS
SHOE, PACKAGING AND HANG TAG
ILLUSTRATION AND PRODUCT DESIGN
USA, 2002

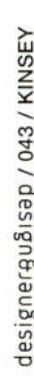

INSTALLATION DISPOZE
GALERIE BLK/MRKT
5 x 3 M
ACRYLIQUE, BOMBE DE PEINTURE ET HUILE SUR DES OBJETS TROUVÉS
LOS ANGELES, 2003

DISPOZE INSTALLATION
BLK/MRKT GALLERY
16' x 9'
ACRYLIC, SPRAY PAINT AND OIL ON FOUND OBJECTS
LOS ANGELES, 2003

SCULPTURAL MUFAL – GALERIE BLK/MRKT
3 x 2 M
ACRYLIQUE, BOMEE DE PEINTURE ET HUILE SUR DES OBJETS TFOUVÉS
LOS ANGELES, 2003

SCULPTURAL MURAL – BLK/MRKT GALLERY
12' x 7'
ACRYLIC, SPRAY PAINT AND OIL ON FOUND OBJECTS
LOS ANGELES, 2003

EXPIRE
05 02
EXP.
25
3602

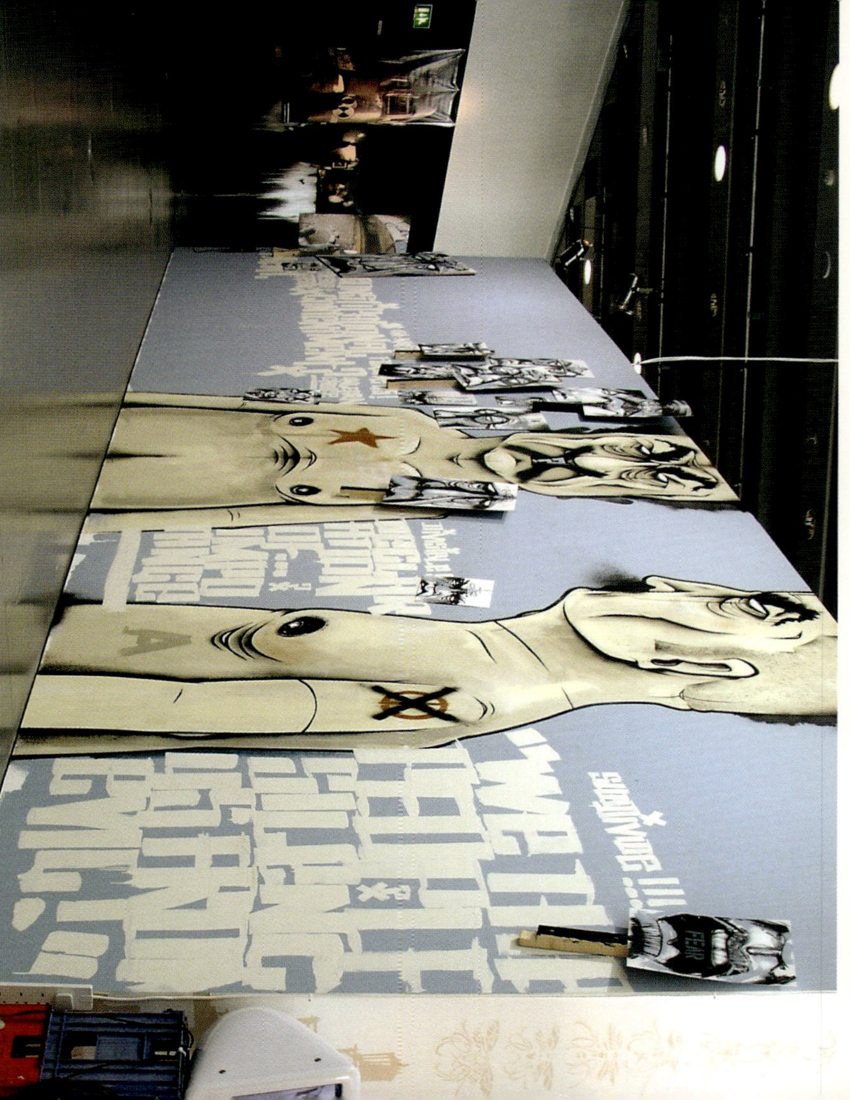

INSTALLATION ILL COMMUNICATION
URBIS MUSEUM
4 x 18 M
ACRYLIQUE, PAPIER, BOMBE DE PEINTURE ET HUILE
ANGLETERRE, 2004

ILL COMMUNICATION INSTALLATION
URBIS MUSEUM
15' x 60'
ACRYLIC, PAPER, SPRAY PAINT AND OIL
ENGLAND, 2004

INSTALLATION ILL COMMUNICATION
URBIS MUSEUM
4 x 9 M ACRYLIQUE, BOMBE DE PEINTURE
ET HUILE
ANGLETERRE, 2004

ILL COMMUNICATION INSTALLATION
URBIS MUSEUM
15' x 30' ACRYLIC, SPRAY PAINT AND OIL
ENGLAND, 2004

HOTEL DES ARTS
4 x 4 x 3 M
ACRYLIQUE, PAPIER, BOMBE DE PEINTURE
ET HUILE
SAN FRANCISCO, 2005

HOTEL DES ARTS
15' x 15' x 9'
ACRYLIC, PAPER, SPRAY PAINT AND OIL
SAN FRANCISCO, 2005

脱勉強
unlea

STICKERS SÉRIGRAPHIÉS
ÉTATS-UNIS, 1998-2004

SCREEN PRINTED STICKERS
USA, 1998-2004

DOME
61 x 45 CM
SÉRIGRAPHIE SUR PAPIER
ÉTATS-UNIS, 1999

DOME
24" x 18"
SCREEN PRINT ON PAPER
USA, 1999

UNLEARN
TAUGHT BELIEVED MISLED MOLDED PURSUED

SUFFOCATE
ILLUSTRATION
ÉTATS-UNIS, 1998

SUFFOCATE
ILLUSTRATION
USA, 1998

HEADBACK JAPAN
45 x 61 CM
SÉRIGRAPHIE SUR PAPIER
ÉTATS-UNIS, 2001

HEADBACK JAPAN
18" x 24"
SCREEN PRINT ON PAPER
USA, 2001

AFFICHE DE L'EXPOSITION KINSEY & MAMBO
« MESSAGE FROM THE SOUL »
GALERIE MAGDA DANYSZ
90 x 45 CM
SÉRIGRAPHIE SUR PAPIER
FRANCE, 2001

KINSEY & MAMBO "MESSAGE FROM THE
SOUL" EXHIBITION PRINT
MAGDA DANYSZ GALLERY
36" x 18"
SCREEN PRINT ON PAPER
FRANCE, 2001

VISUAL SNIPERS
CLIENT : BLK/MRKT
90 x 61 CM
SÉRIGRAPHIE SUR PAPIER
ÉTATS-UNIS, 1998

VISUAL SNIPERS
CLIENT: BLK/MRKT
36" x 24"
SCREEN PRINT ON PAPER
USA, 1998

VISUAL SNIPER SQUAD
CLIENT : BLK/MRKT
60 x 45 CM
SÉRIGRAPHIE SUR PAPIER
ÉTATS-UNIS, 2000

VISUAL SNIPER SQUAD
CLIENT: BLK/MRKT
24" x 18"
SCREEN PRINT ON PAPER
USA, 2000

BLKMRKT.COM
BLKMRKT INC.
VISUAL SNIPER SQUAD
INNOVATIVE MIXTURES - CREATIVE APPLICATION
DESIGN-BRANDING-CONCEPTS-ART
2000
BLK/MRKT
CREATIVE VISUAL COMMUNICATION
BLK/MRKT INC.

MONTRES CONÇUES PAR KINSEY
POUR LE 100E ANNIVERSAIRE DE TIMEX
ILLUSTRATION ET DESIGN
ÉTATS-UNIS, 2004

KINSEY SIGNATURE WATCHES FOR TIMEX'S
100TH ANNIVERSARY
ILLUSTRATION AND PRODUCT DESIGN
USA, 2004

Future Soul ~ Polyrhythms ~ Progressive World ~ Live Construct

AZTEKSOL

¡Sin Fronteras!

FLYER AZTEKSOL
CLIENT : DJ GAGE
ILLUSTRATION ET DESIGN
ÉTATS-UNIS, 1999

AZTEKSOL FLYER
CLIENT: DJ GAGE
ILLUSTRATION AND DESIGN
USA, 1999

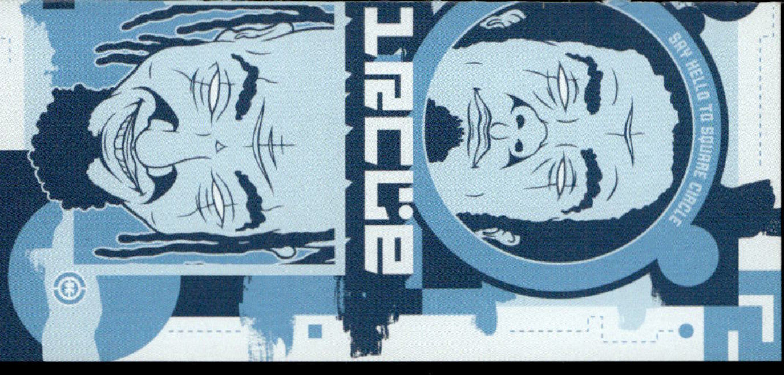

SQUARE CIRCLE « SAY HELLO TO SQUARE CIRCLE »
CLIENT : REVOLT RECORDS
LOGO, POCHETTE DE CD ET PACKAGING
ILLUSTRATION ET DESIGN GRAPHIQUE
ÉTATS-UNIS, 2001

SQUARE CIRCLE "SAY HELLO TO SQUARE CIRCLE"
CLIENT: REVOLT RECORDS
LOGO, CD COVER AND PACKAGING
ILLUSTRATION AND DESIGN
USA, 2001

SONDRE LERCHE « DAYS THAT ARE OVER »
CLIENT : VIRGIN RECORDS, NORWAY
LOGO, POCHETTE DE CD ET PACKAGING
NORWAY, 2004

SONDRE LERCHE "DAYS THAT ARE OVER"
CLIENT: VIRGIN RECORDS, NORWAY
LOGO, CD COVER AND PACKAGING
NORWAY, 2004

SONDRE LERCHE « TWO WAY MONOLAUGE »
CLIENT : VIRGIN RECORDS, NORWAY
LOGO, POCHETTE DE CD ET PACKAGING
NORWAY, 2004

SONDRE LERCHE "TWO WAY MONOLAUGE"
CLIENT: VIRGIN RECORDS, NORWAY
LOGO, CD COVER AND PACKAGING
NORWAY, 2004

DJ SPOOKY "RIDDIM WARFARE"
CLIENT: ASPHODEL RECORDS
LOGO, CD COVER AND PACKAGING
USA, 1998

DJ SPOOKY « RIDDIM WARFARE »
CLIENT : ASPHODEL RECORDS
LOGO, POCHETTE DE CD ET PACKAGING
ÉTATS-UNIS, 1998

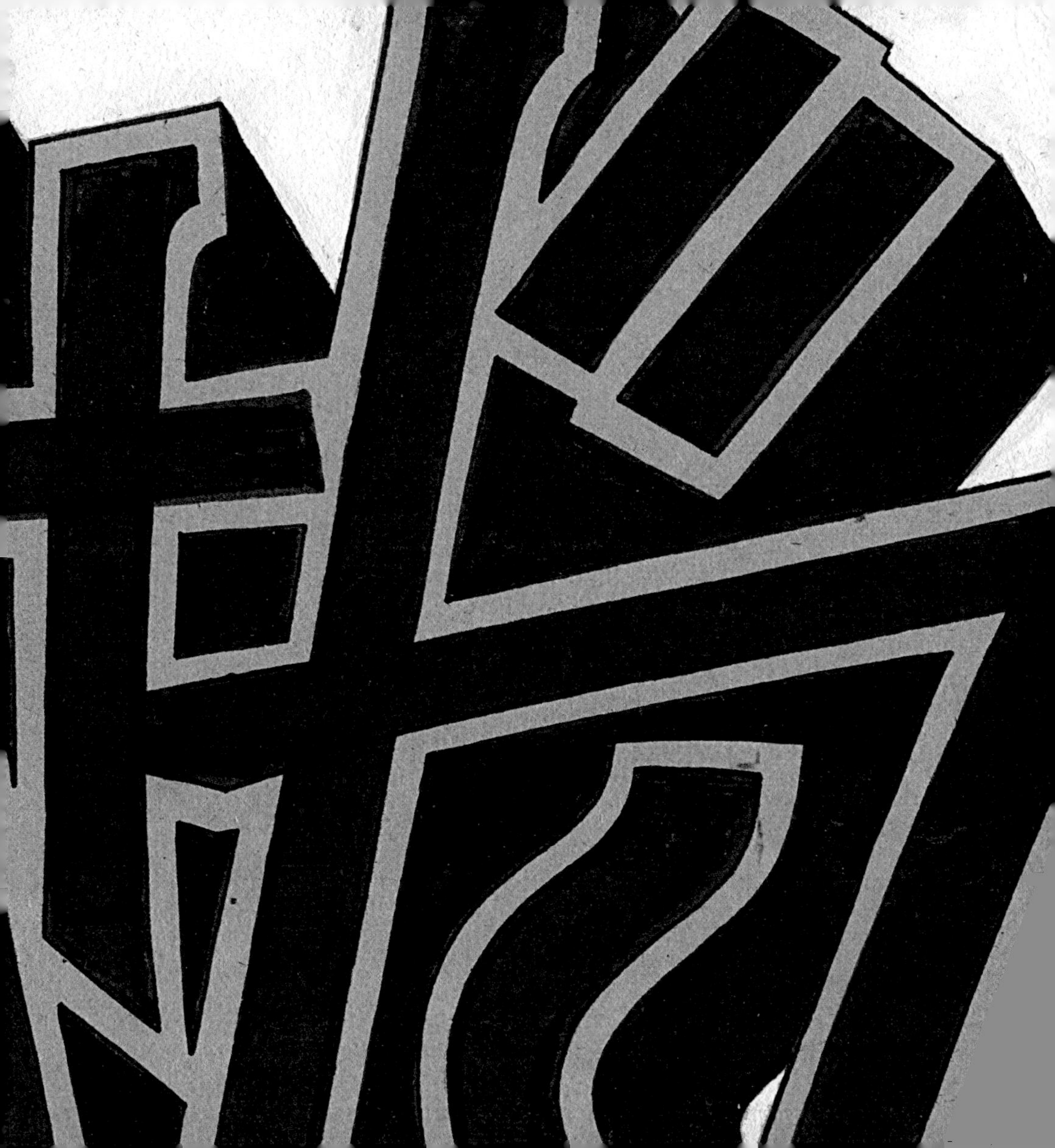

PAGES 110-111 :
PARIS FREESTYLE « BÜST »
20 x 25 CM
ACRYLIQUE, STYLO ET ENCRE SUR CARTON
ÉTATS-UNIS, 2001

PAGES 110-11:
PARIS FREESTYLE "BÜST"
8" x 10" ACRYLIC WITH PEN AND INK
ON CHIPBOARD
USA, 2001

MASK & BLOCKHEAD
(DE GAUCHE À DROITE)
SÉRIGRAPHIE
ÉTATS-UNIS, 2003

MASK & BLOCKHEAD
(LEFT TO RIGHT)
SCREEN PRINTING
USA, 2003

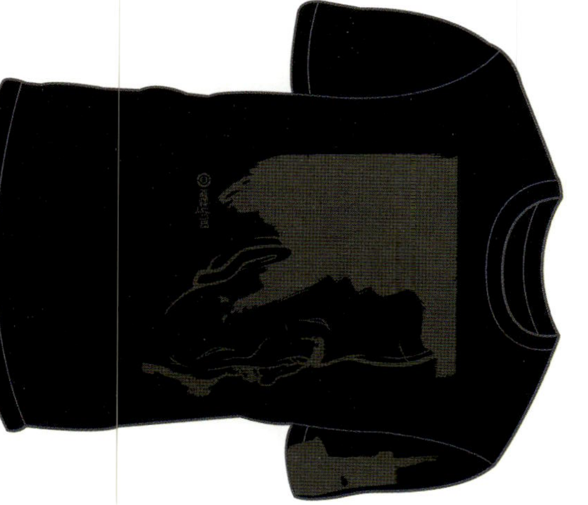

PARIS FREESTYLE
SÉRIGRAPHIE
ÉTATS-UNIS, 2002

PARIS FREESTYLE
SCREEN PRINTING
USA, 2002

PARIS . FRANCE

EXPEDITION ONE LOGO
CORPORATE IDENTITY
USA, 1996

LOGO EXPEDITION ONE
IDENTITÉ VISUELLE
ÉTATS-UNIS, 1996

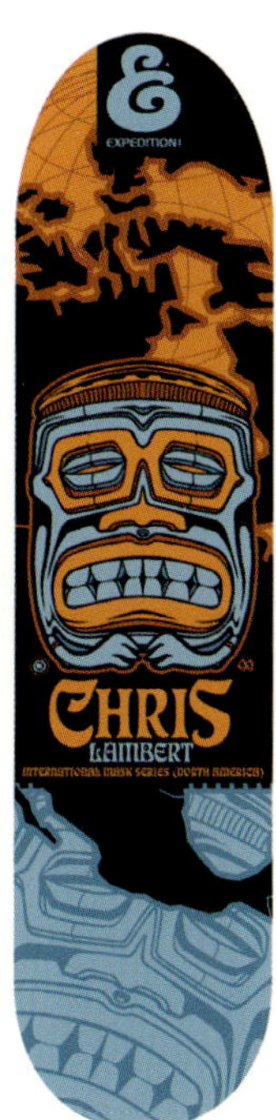

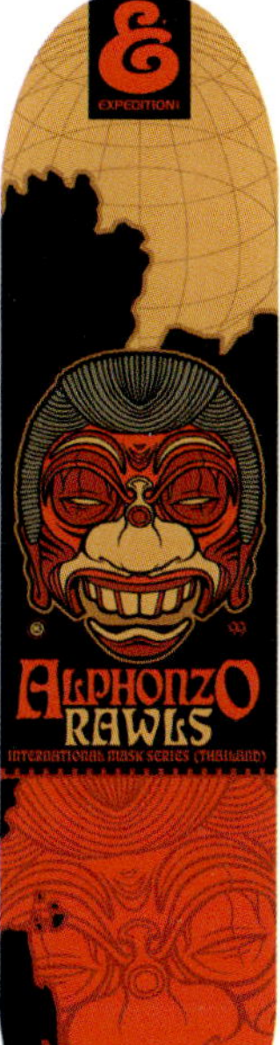

MASK SERIES
CLIENT : EXPEDITION ONE SKATEBOARDS
SKATEBOARDS SÉRIGRAPHIÉS
ÉTATS-UNIS, 1999

MASK SERIES
CLIENT: EXPEDITION ONE SKATEBOARDS
SCREEN PRINTED BOARDS
USA, 1999

PERSONNAGES CONÇUS PAR KINSEY
CLIENT : ADFUNTURE WORKSHOP
PERSONNAGES MOULÉS EN CAOUTCHOUC
HONG KONG, 2004

KINSEY SIGNATURE CHARACTERS
CLIENT: ADFUNTURE WORKSHOP
VINYL MOLDED CHARACTERS
HONG KONG, 2004

EDUCATION

Art Institute of Atlanta, May 1993, Associates Degree, Illustration & Design
Art Institute of Pittsburgh, Fall 1989

GUEST SPEAKINGS

Art Center Pasadena – artist presentation and studio visit, September 2005
UCLA Design class, Los Angeles – artist presentation and studio visit, June 2005
AIGA Los Angeles – artist presentation and studio visit, October 2004
Modart Munich, Germany – student workshop & guest speaking, February 2003
University of Florida – Ligature Design conference. Guest speaking and presentation to graduating classes, March 2001
Art Institute of Atlanta – Graduating class review, June 1993

SOLO EXHIBITIONS

BLK/MRKT Gallery, Los Angeles, September 2006
Alice BXL, Belgium, April 2006
The Outside Institute, London, Spring 2006
Boon Gallery, Salem, Mass., December 2005
Travis Parker, San Diego, November 2003
Basil Hayward Gallery – Kinsey at Powell's, Portland, October 2003
BLK/MRKT Gallery, Los Angeles, April 2003
Magda Danysz Gallery, Paris, April 2001
381G Gallery, San Francisco, March 2000
ARO.SPACE, Seattle, August 1999

GROUP EXHIBITIONS

Keep A Breast, New York & Los Angeles, October 2005
Low Gallery – Grand opening, San Francisco, November 2004
Urbis Museum – Ill Communication, Manchester, England, July – October 2004
Yerba Buena Arts Center – Beautiful Losers, San Francisco, March – October 2004
The Lab 101 – Streewise 3, Los Angeles, April 2004
NY Arts Gallery – Decipher 2.0, New York, August 2003
ModArt3, Munich, Germany, February, 2003
This is me – Traveling Group show, Tokyo, Los Angeles, New York, Paris & London, June 2002
222 Gallery – Separations, Philadelphia, August 2002
Apart Gallery – Streetwise 2, London, July 2002
Compound Gallery – Andy Howell and Dave Kinsey, Portland, October 2002
Revoluciones – The Four Horseman, Denver, April 2002
Alife – Arkitip Exhibition 003, New York, June 2001
Magda Danysz Gallery – Mambo and Kinsey, Paris, April 2001
Plush Gallery – Jonze, Dallas, July 2000
La Panaderia Gallery, Mexico City, November 1999
Carnation Building – ModArt2, San Diego, September 1999
Workhorse Studios Gallery – New Blood, Baltimore, November 1998
Army Street Gallery, San Francisco, May 1998
IP Gallery – BLK/MRKT show, San Diego, December 1998
Underground Gallery, Atlanta, June 1995

PUBLICATIONS

HANDMADE – Italy, January 2006; Designer feature / **DPI MAGAZINE** – Hong Kong, Volume 77; Artist feature / **TERRITORY MAGAZINE** – Malaysia, Issue 04; Artist feature / **NEW YORK TIMES** – New York, July 10th 2005; Art featured / **SEARCH MEGAZINE** – Portugal, Summer 2005; Cover design & artist feature / **JUXTAPOZ** – San Francisco, March 2005; B&W issue, Art featured / **VINYL WILL KILL** – Germany, January 2005; Artist feature / **CAP & DESIGN** – Stockholm, Issue no. 8, November 2004; Artist feature / **VOX** – Russia, Issue 02, Spring 2004; Artist feature / **STREETWEAR TODAY** – Germany, Spring 2004; Cover design & artist feature / **DEFRAG** – Italy, Spring 2004; Artist feature / **WIRED** – San Francisco, Issue 12-03, March 2004; Cover design / **ART PROSTITUTE** – Dallas, Issue 3, Fall 2003; Artist feature / **BLACK BOOK** – New York, Issue 29, Fall 2003; Contributing art / **XLR8R** – San Francisco, Issue 67 Spring 2003; Agency review / **STRAIGHT NO CHASER** – London, Issue 27, October 2003; Artist feature / **JUICE** – Munich, Germany, Fall 2003, Artist feature / **PICTOPLASMA 2** – Berlin, 2003; Featured illustrations / **WORD** – Zurich, Fall 2003 Issue 15; Cover Illustration & artist feature / **WARP** – Japan, Volume 6, Issue 84 2003; Artist feature / **BOREDOM** – Berlin, 2003 Artist Collective published by Scott Morrison; Illustration / **ANTHEM** – Los Angeles, Fall 2002 Issue 007; Artist feature / **TRACE** – New York, Issue 36, Fall 2002; Artist feature / **MERCURY** – Portland, 2002 issue vol. 3 no. 20; Cover design & artist feature / **TRANSMISSION 2** – Singapore, 2002 published by Phunk Studio; Artist feature / **NYLON** – New York, April 2002 issue; Fashion illustrations & artist feature / **STYLE & THE FAMILY TUNES** – Berlin, 2001 Issue 38; Illustration spread / **LODOWN BOOK 2 – SCHIZOPHRENIC** – Berlin, 2001; Illustration spreads / **SKY-H** – Hong Kong, 2001; Artist feature / **BLOWER** – London, Published 2001 Booth-Clibborn Editions Limited; Artist feature / **DESIGN IS KINKY** – Sydney, 2001; Illustration spreads / **BEAUTIFUL DECAY** – Baltimore, 2001 Premier issue; Artist feature / **ANTHEM** – Los Angeles, Fall 2001 issue 004; Cover design & artist feature / **BLAST** – Paris, April 2001 issue #15; Artist feature. / **ARKITIP** – Los Angeles, 2000 issue #5; Illustration spreads / **URB** – Los Angeles, September 2000 issue; Artist feature / **SLAP MAGAZINE** – San Francisco January 2000 issue; Artist feature / **SKRAWL – DIRTY GRAPHICS & STRANGE CHARACTERS** – London, 1999; Featured design / **SUGAR** – Paris, May 1999 issue; Artist feature / **MATIZ** – Mexico City, February 1999 issue 18; Artist feature / **LODOWN BOOK #1 – GRAPHIC ENGINEERING** – Berlin, 1998; Illustrations featured in “Best of Issues” / **TRANSWORLD SKATEBOARDING** – San Diego, May 1995 issue; Artist feature / **THE UNIVERSITY REPORTER** – Atlanta, Issue 2:3 October 1993; Cover illustration.

SPECIAL THANKS:

My lovely Jana, George Trumbull, Shana Nys Dambrot, Céline Remechido and Pyramyd publishing, Mambo & everyone who has supported my artistic journey.

FOR MORE INFO:

kinseyvisual.com and blkmrkt.com